FULL STEAM AHEAD

Welcome to this celebration of the golden age of steam train travel - past, present and future. The mainline steam era started in North West England in 1830, with the opening of the Liverpool & Manchester Railway, and ended here in 1968 with British Railways' last scheduled passenger train "the Fifteen Guinea Special" from Liverpool to Carlisle via Manchester.

Now 41 years on we are in the incredible situation of being able to offer regularly timetabled mainline steam trains from Liverpool Lime Street for the second summer running. The inaugural trip for the Live Steam from Lime Street 2009 programme, on July 4, will be our first to Scarborough, followed by others to Carlisle, Holyhead and the York Yule-tide Express on December 13.

Last year the excursions, organised by the Liverpool Daily Post & Echo, in partnership with National Museums Liverpool and the Railway Touring Company, defied our expectations and sold out.

We hope to build on that success this year, not only with haulage by last summer's stalwart septuagenerians Princess Elizabeth and Union of South Africa, but bolstered by Duchess of Sutherland and, making its mainline return after 47 years, Royal Scot.

This book aims to convey a flavour of last year's trains and give a taste of what will come, through the engines, personalities and routes. We also look back at yesterday's steam age and its trains, stations and people who created the rich legacy we enjoy today.

Whether you can join us on the trains, lulled by the rhythm of the track, or remain an armchair traveller with smoke trails drifting through the corners of your mind, we hope you will take pleasure in this steamy journey of pictures and words.

PETER ELSON,
LIVERPOOL DAILY POST & ECHO

A First Class Train, with the Mail.

A Second Class Train for Passengers.

A Train of Waggons with Goods &c.

A Train of Carriages with Cattle.

RAILWAY CONVEYANCES FROM LIVERPOOL TO MANCHESTER.

London. Published 1834, by Ackermann & Co. 96 Strand.

My thanks to the hundreds of people, both paid and voluntary,
who have made our Live Steam from Lime Street trips and this book a reality.
These include staff at The Railway Touring Company, Locomotive 6201 Princess Elizabeth
Society Limited, The Princess Royal Class Locomotive Trust (Duchess of Sutherland), John
Cameron's Union of South Africa, Bressingham Steam Museum (Royal Scot),
Ian Riley & Son (E) Ltd (The Lancashire Fusilier), A1 Class Locomotive Trust (Tornado), West
Coast Railway, Riviera Trains, Network Rail, Premier Catering, National Railway Museum,
St Helens Council Tourism Development, Rainhill Railway & Heritage Society.
Finally, my gratitude to Trinity Mirror's Sports Media's designers, also to Claire Rider, of
National Museums Liverpool, (whose original idea the steam train season was)
and Stephen Done for his unstinting support.

LIVERPOOL AND MANCHESTER RAILWAY

The Liverpool & Manchester Railway was the world's first, purpose-built, double track intercity railway.

Built to carry raw materials for the textile industry imported through Liverpool, it revolutionised transport across the globe and ushered in the modern, technological age. An instant success for passenger travel, too, it forced upon the populous what Merseyside historian Patrick Moran dubbed "the tyranny of the timetable".

The L&MR's progressive directors thought of using steam locomotive power from the start. This view was not unopposed. These were still early days in the industrial revolution and steam locomotives had their limitations. They were less powerful and less reliable than they were to become.

There was also opposition from the public and local authorities. In spite of this, there was a wave of well-intentioned advice on how to tackle the motive power problem. L&MR treasurer, Henry Booth, whose house still stands in Rodney Street, Liverpool, described the dilemma.

"Multifarious were the schemes proposed to the directors for facilitating locomotion. The difficulty was to choose and decide," he said.

With construction of the line well underway from 1828, the need to decide on the competing claims of power faced the directors.

Should it be horse power, stationary engines (built at the lineside with cables to haul the trains) or self-propelled steam engines (ie. locomotives)?

Statue of Henry Booth at St George's Hall

A delegation was sent to study the traction methods on the Stockton & Darlington Railway, a goods line opened in 1825. Plenty of data was amassed, but no final conclusion reached. While with hindsight, it might seem that steam locomotives were the obvious solution, it was the newest and largely untested alternative.

In fact, the well-established stationary engine technology of rope-haulage and winding systems seemed ideal for the route's many gradients.

A locomotive called Twin Sisters was ordered from Robert Stephenson (son of engineer George and already an established steam engine builder) for evaluation. Stephenson made a plea to the directors on April 20, 1829, emphasising the shortcomings of horses and fixed engines.

As a result, the board proposed the Rainhill Trials competition, open to all forms of motive power and with a prize of £500. It took place on a level stretch of the newly-laid railway, east of Rainhill, starting on October 5, 1829.

Keith Naylor, St Helens railway historian says: "The most important stipulation was that entrants should run 40 times over the one and three-quarter mile secton to simulate a distance equivalent to 70 miles. That is Liverpool to Manchester and return with some to spare".

Speed must be no less than 10mph and the power units must be able to pull three times their own weight.

The most notable competitors were Rocket, designed by George Stephenson and built by his son's firm, Robert Stephenson & Co, of Newcastle upon Tyne; Novelty, built by John Braithwaite and John Ericsson, of London; the heavyweight Sans Pareil, built by Timothy Hackworth, of Darlington; and Perseverance, by Timothy Burstall, of Leith.

Unfortunately, the latter was damaged in transit to Rainhill.

With several years of planning and building already complete, local interest had reached fever pitch and engineers from Europe and the US attended the trials.

The main competitors at Rainhill for the 1829 trials courtesy of Rainhill Railway Museum and Library

More than 10,000 spectators lined the testing route on the first day, before getting down to seriously enjoying themselves in marquees and local taverns.

Day one, on Tuesday, October 6, was really only a warm-up, yet Rocket lived up to its name and achieved 24mph, only to be topped by Novelty at 28mph.

Sans Pareil made one outing and Thomas Shaw Brandreth's horse-powered Cycloped pulled 50 people at 5mph.

The even more bizarre two man-powered Manumotive carried six passengers, "with no great velocity" sneered The Times.

Day two, Wednesday, was far more intense and less of a public knees-up, but bad weather reduced the site to a mud-bath.

Novelty ran up to 20mph, before its ashpan draught bellows burst. Brandreth's Cycloped self-destructed when its horse fell through the floor (but was not injured).

Thursday was the most testing day, with Rocket steaming for 20 journeys (ie 35 miles) in three hours 12 minutes and reducing this to two hours 57 minutes.

Hauling 13 tons of loaded wagons to match the trials' load conditions, Rocket averaged 12.5mph. Without a load, its highest speed was 29mph.

Liverpool & Manchester Centenary celebrations at Wavertree, Liverpool, organised by the London & Scottish Railway, in 1930

The people's choice, Novelty, pulled in the crowds on Saturday. After a dispute with the directors and a burst feed-pipe were sorted out, it sped up to 30mph, only for Rocket to outpace it at 32mph. On Tuesday, October 13, Sans Pareil performed eight trips with its heavy load at more than 16mph, until it was defeated by a failed water pump.

The next day Perseverance and Novelty were disqualified when they both blew boiler joints. This caused a minor contretemps as Novelty's parts were supplied by Robert Stephenson & Co, but no sabotage was proved, or was likely.

Rocket, driven by Robert Stephenson, rose to a bravura final flourish, storming up the 1-in-96 incline approaching Rainhill, with a full load at 12mph. The £500 trials prize thus went to the Stephensons and Henry Booth. Of course, the canny Geordies had specifically tailored Rocket's design to the trials' rules.

The prize also ensured they received the contracts for the line's first generation of locomotives at Robert Stephenson's Forth Street works in Newcastle.

The company produced steam locomotives in use until the end of mainline steam in 1968, a fitting tribute to the Stephensons who, therefore, were involved from first to last.

KEEPER OF THE STEAM AGE FLAME

Above: Andrew Scott
director of the
National Railway
Museum in York, with
Flying Scotsman

IT'S the Valhalla of the steam age, the railway heaven in which the pantheon of greats like Mallard, Flying Scotsman and City of Truro live on forever.

But it's also the repository of serious academic information about railways and the most popular museum in Britain outside of London.

This is the National Railway Museum, in York, under the direction of Andrew Scott.

Being in charge of the world's biggest railway museum is a huge privilege and Andrew seems relaxed about juggling its sometimes conflicting demands.

"It's one of the great things that this museum works on many levels. This is a hugely popular free tourist attraction where people come to soak themselves in the steam age," says Andrew.

"But we are also an academic institute with considerable depth to our archives, which allows us to range from schools' visits to welcoming scholars to our new post graduate resource centre.

"One of the great joys for me is that not only do we get the expected men of a certain age who are keen on steam trains, but we also attract young people and women. They also record high levels of visitor satisfaction."

This is a matter they take very seriously, working hard with the help of a planning manager to maintain and develop visitor interest with the younger generation.

"You must help youngsters to comprehend why the railway age was so important, as their level of received understanding is much lower than that of the older generation, whose lives embraced railways more," says Andrew.

"We have the giants of the steam age here and can tell the story of railways in buckets, thanks also to all our incredible memorabilia."

This helps to explain how railways began long before the steam age. It also illustrates how steam then brought cheap mechanical transport to the world for the first time.

"While life has moved on from the railway age, it has shaped the world we live in today, with cheap food always available and the choice of travelling when and where we want to go. All this came with the railways; before that people rarely moved from their home towns. The railways also lubricated the world's industrialisation."

The Duke of Wellington, victor of Waterloo, straddled the end of the Napoleonic era and the industrial revolution which created our modern nations.

"It all kicked off at the point when Wellington, by now prime minister, opened the Liverpool & Manchester Railway in 1830 and embarked on his historic journey between the two cities," says Andrew.

The NRM has a very generous and wide-ranging policy of loans, even to the extent of trusting preservation groups with restoring locomotives into working order.

"We've always thought of York as the headquarters of the collection and we'd be in dead trouble if everyone returned everything to us!" laughs Andrew.

Britain is blessed with having a powerful, well-organised volunteer heritage railway workforce with whom the NRM can work.

"People tell us it's not good enough to look at cold locomotives in a museum, so in partnership with the railway heritage sector we can get some of them steaming. Given that we have 100 locomotives, it's reasonable that some should operate, and we currently have eight in steam," says Andrew.>>>

Above: The Great Hall at the National Railway Museum in York, with Eurostar, Mallard and Rocket replica

Below: A young enthausiast at the NRM

>>> Some locomotives will never steam, such as the remains of the original Rocket, which is too precious a national asset to alter. It is vital that physical evidence of such an early locomotive is undisturbed.

The fine Edwardian express locomotive Lode Star will be kept as it is, an example of a 1950 restoration by the former Great Western Railway's finest craftsmen at its Swindon birthplace. It is a different matter with a modern steam locomotive like Oliver Cromwell, built at Crewe in 1951. Restoration was largely funded by a Steam Railway magazine campaign.

"This locomotive is already giving a huge amount of enjoyment to the public all over the country with a volunteer team caring for it, but we can't use taxpayers' money to do this," says Andrew.

In contrast, the highly popular Green Arrow's boiler certificate has expired. This scaled down Flying Scotsman is unlikely to steam again because the costly and extensive rebuild would compromise its historical integrity, believes Andrew.

The world steam speed-holder Mallard was restored to working order in the 1980s, but is now static, as it is thought to be the crucial locomotive every visitor wants to see in situ.

The Museum also is involved with the future of British mainline steam and played a vital part to help build the brand new Peppercorn A1 class locomotive Tornado, using both its practical skills and the latest technological archiving systems.

"Not only was York the final home of the Peppercorn class A1s, but the original drawings used to recreate this extinct class of steam locomotive are preserved in the NRM's archive centre Search Engine," says Andrew.

"Without the Museum's involvement in hosting the locomotive during her main line trials and providing painting facilities this fantastic project probably would not have been possible. We're very excited to see Tornado, which is a credit to everyone involved."

Steam our Scotsman appeal

Blessed with a name that grips the imagination, Flying Scotsman (above) is one steam locomotive which will never be preserved in aspic.

The supremely elegant A3 class locomotive, designed by Sir Nigel Gresley, was the first steam engine to officially surpass 100mph.

The National Railway Museum is undertaking a massive restoration to return the locomotive to full mainline working order. It has launched a Steam Our Scotsman appeal and raised £64,000 so far from members of the public.

As its 85-year working life dictated regular replacement of parts both major and minor, the Museum feels nothing of the original is being lost.

"Scotsman is at the other end of the spectrum from Rocket. It's the flagship of the steam era and will be the last engine steaming after all the others have finished," says Andrew Scott, head of the NRM.

"But the cost of the current overhaul is frightening, around £1m, and we're trying to raise £150,000 to fit vacuum brakes so it can run with old rolling stock on the private preserved railway lines.

"It seems like a bottomless pit, but we're heartened by 6,000 individual donations from the public and the fact that this is the long-needed thorough overhaul that will allow Scotsman to run for many more years."

EDGE HILL NATIONAL RAILWAY MUSEUM?

Can a museum suffer from having too many artefacts of national and international significance?

When such a problem beset the National Railway Museum, it invested in a splendid satellite museum called Locomotion, at Shildon, Co Durham.

Such is its success that Andrew Scott, director of the NRM, is actively looking for other sites around the country, particularly those of historical railway significance.

The NRM still has an embarrassment of rail riches in store, so the amazing deal is that it will provide the priceless historic contents if local bodies create a suitable building.

Given that Edge Hill is the world's oldest operational railway station and its attractive 1836 buildings are being refurbished for community use, would this not be an ideal location?

Furthermore, alongside this original Liverpool & Manchester Railway station lies the large, postwar concrete skeleton of Edge Hill's former goods transit shed, an ideal framework onto which an exciting new museum could be grafted.

"We were lucky in finding a super local authority, Sedgefield Borough Council, which was deeply committed to Locomotion. They made the site and provided the core capital funding," explains Andrew.

The £11m cost of Locomotion The National Railway Museum at Shildon, included £7.5m Heritage Lottery Fund and EU funding.

Surely Liverpool City Council and other North West local government bodies, whose existence is partly derived from the economic vision of the builders of the Liverpool & Manchester Railway, won't be able to resist such a challenge?

Boarded up for decades, Edge Hill station was an affront to its historic importance as a major surviving relic of the Liverpool & Manchester Railway.

Thankfully now it has a new lease of life after being designated as one of three cultural "pavilions" created for Liverpool's 2008 Capital of Culture.

Experimental arts organisation Metal Culture, founded by Liverpool-born artistic director Jude Kelly, is transforming the two fine 1836 station buildings on their island platforms.

The plans by Liverpool architects Shed KM involve turning the unused Grade II-listed station in Tunnel Road into studio space for 16 artists, galleries and performance areas.

The attractive Rainhill railway station buildings from 1842 also cry out for a new lease of life. This might be resolved courtesy of St Helens Council's plans for a new Rainhill Trials railway museum there.

The L&MR's handsome eastern terminus of Manchester Liverpool Road is fully restored as part of Manchester Museum of Science and Industry.

In full daily use are features along the line like the Rainhill skew bridge, carrying heavier traffic than ever on the A57 and Sankey viaduct, the world's first ever railway viaduct.

Surely now is the time to lobby for the L&MR to become a World Heritage Site? No other geographical area has influenced the modern world as much as this one.

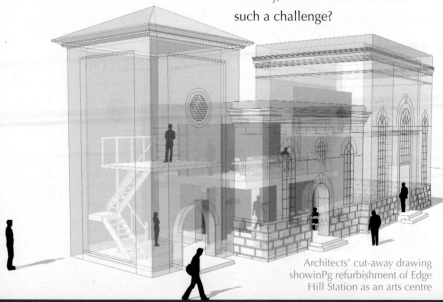

Architects' cut-away drawing showinPg refurbishment of Edge Hill Station as an arts centre

RAINHILL TRIALS VIRTUAL MUSEUM

Rainhill's claim to be the birthplace of the railways has gone global, courtesy of new technology.

It is said that the colossal impact of the railways 180 years ago is echoed by the changes wrought by the internet today.

So harnessing modern computer technology to build a virtual museum to showcase the world-changing Rainhill Trials, is particularly fitting.

The Rainhill Trials Virtual Museum has been created by St Helens Council, aided by Rainhill Railway and Heritage Society, to service a growing worldwide interest in the 1829 event.

It is hoped the Rainhill Trials Virtual Museum will become the definitive destination for information about the trials, by using a mixture of interactive technology and video on-line, designed by Zut Media, a local multi-media company.

The site gives a stimulating on-line commemoration of the locomotive trials, including on-line personal guides, a user-forum, films, and audio-visual interviews with local experts and rail enthusiasts.

David Gavin, St Helens Council regeneration projects manager, says: "While we managed the project, it's been delivered from local people and the Rainhill Railway and Heritage Society.

" This is the first website dedicated to the trials and is our first stage in creating something officially meaningful."

The second stage will investigate relocating the Rainhill Railway Museum, which is currently part of Rainhill Library and occupies a 1957-built bogie baggage coach.

The obvious place is Rainhill railway station, a handsome and historic 1842 structure in a perilous state propped up by scaffolding, adjacent to the world's first skew arch, still carrying the busy A57 trunk road.

There is also pressure from local enthusiasts to move the station's redundant Edwardian signal box from its isolated position onto the platform.

"The beauty of the Virtual Museum is that it's low maintenance and open 24 hours a day," says John Whaling, St Helens tourism development manager.

"Further commemorative activity could be located at Rainhill station, subject to the building's state, funding and further investigative work, plus integration with a retail outlet, like a cafe or shop."

Chris Tigwell, vice-chairman of Rainhill Railway and Heritage Society, says: "The Rainhill Trials took place at a time when the highest speed for people was no more than that of a galloping horse.

"It took six hours to get from Liverpool to Manchester by the fastest stage coach, with 10 passengers aboard.

Right: Replica of Stephensons Rocket taking part in a re-enactment of the famous Rainhill trials in 1980 on the 150th anniversary of the original event

Above: Stylish ladies and gentlemen view the Rocket at Rainhill, beneath the famous skew bridge (both designed by George Stephenson) the latter still carrying traffic on the A57 today. Petrie painting courtesy of Rainhill Railway Museum and Library

"The Liverpool & Manchester Railway was about industrial evolution and the attempt by entrepreneurs and inventors to get a steam engine pulling heavy loads up hills.

"This reached a climax with the Rainhill Trials, in 1829, to indisputably decide what the L&MR's motive power would be, and the winner was Stephenson's Rocket.

"The L&MR set the standard for the world, exceeding all expectations, and carried 460,000 passengers and earned a total revenue of £80,000 in its first year, three times that forecasted.

"Soon, food and fuel prices fell in cities. Within a decade, trains ran from London to Scotland and Greenwich Mean Time and the postal service were established nationally."

The L&MR remains very much alive and viable as a major trunk route between the two cities it was built to serve. There are calls for it to be made a World Heritage Site.

"The legacy that allows us to travel on trains today dates back to the Rainhill Trials. That's its true significance," says Chris Tigwell.

The Rainhill Trials Virtual Museum is at www.rainhilltrials.com

Craftsmen at Robert Stephenson and Co complete a replica of Stephensons Rocket for Henry Ford's transport museum in Detroit in 1929, after display on Liverpool Plateau, it was shipped to the USA

TITANS OF THE STEAM AGE

PATHFINDING GIANTS OF THE RAILWAY AGE

George Stephenson 'Father of the railways"

THE son of illiterate parents, the self-educated civil and mechanical engineer George Stephenson was hailed as the "father of the railways" after building the world's first railway to use steam locomotives - the Liverpool & Manchester.

His railway gauge of four feet eight and a half inches (allegedly based on the width of Roman chariot tracks) became the world's standard gauge.

Having paid to study at night school, he was praised by the Victorian establishment as an example of "diligent application" with a "thirst for improvement".

Born in 1781, at Wylam, near Newcastle, he started work controlling pit winding gear, but showed a natural expertise in maintaining colliery pumping gear and was soon promoted.

Richard Trevithick, credited with building the first locomotive in 1804, later constructed one on Tyneside. This inspired Stephenson to build Blucher, in 1814, for Killingworth Colliery. This was the first successful flange-wheel adhesion locomotive, ie its own weight gave enough grip to haul a train.

The proposed Stockton & Darlington Railway planned to use horse-drawn carts, but Stephenson persuaded its board to adopt steam power and surveyed the line in 1821 assisted by his 18-year-old son Robert.

The Stephensons set up a locomotive works Robert Stephenson & Co, in Newcastle, to make the motive power for the line, which was opened amid great fanfare in 1825.

Noting how even small inclines decelerated steam locomotives and declines rendered their brakes useless, George advocated level alignments.

He deployed this on engineering the L&MR, necessitating his phenomenal of achievements of floating the line across the seemingly bottomless Chat Moss peat bog, building the Sankey viaduct (a world first and endlessly replicated everywhere) and Rainhill skew arch (likewise).

George was besieged with work, but after a decade his conservative views of engineering meant he was regarded as a safe pair of hands, rather than a pioneer.

The mantle of cutting-edge railway engineering passed to his only son Robert, his pupil Joseph Locke and their friend Isambard Kingdom Brunel.

Many of the achievements credited to George (who died in 1848) were really the combined work of father and son.

Robert Stephenson who built the Britainnia Bridge over the Menai

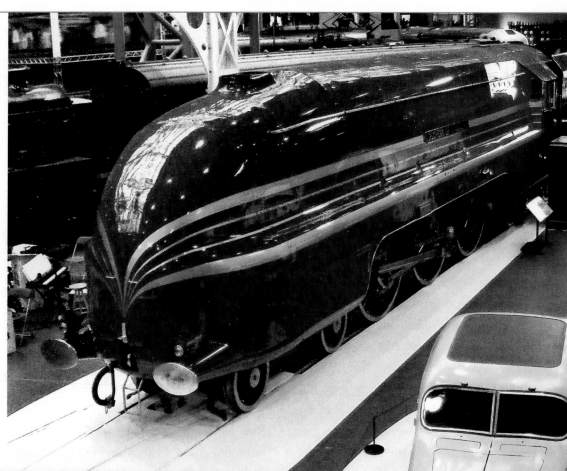

Right: The duchess in NRM's streamlined styling an Era with Chrysler air flow car

THE OTHER LADY HAMILTON

A BOLD NEW PROJECT RESTORED A FORMER
EDGE HILL FAVOURITE TO ITS ORIGINAL
ART DECO SPLENDOUR FOR A NEW GENERATION

THE sale of Halewood car plant to an Indian company helped to restore the amazing appearance of a famous Liverpool steam locomotive.

When the chief executive of the giant Tata industrial company was in Britain to purchase Jaguar Land-Rover he heard that plans to restreamline the Duchess of Hamilton engine suffered a year's delay. This was because the six-foot wide sheets of steel needed to return the Duchess to her original 1938 Crewe-built condition were no longer produced in Britain.

An attempt by the project's chief engineer Bob Meanley to source the steel from China in 2008 was successful - but only if he bought a batch of 10,000 sheets. As a gesture of goodwill, Tata especially rolled the exact number at its Corus subsidiary at Port Talbot, in South Wales.

Duchess of Hamilton was based at Liverpool Edge Hill shed during the early 1960s and daily steamed past the Halewood plant site hauling London expresses.

In another Indian link, the Duchess, one of the celebrated Princess Coronation class, was designed by Sir William Stanier, who advised the Indian government on its railway system.

The Duchess' bullet-nosed look was part of the 1930s streamlining mania. The locomotive was one of 58 built for hauling the new deluxe Coronation Scot high-speed London - Glasgow service and other top-link expresses. It was the culmination of the deadly rivalry between her owners, the London Midland & Scottish Railway and the London North Eastern Railway.

In 1939, Duchess of Hamilton was shipped to the US for exhibition in New York and on tour with new crimson lake coaches for the deluxe Coronation Scot streamlined London - Glasgow express service.

Trapped by the war in the US, the dire need for railway locomotives in Britain meant the Duchess made the dangerous voyage home in 1942 during the Battle of the Atlantic.

The locomotive's streamlining was removed in 1947 for easier maintainance in the postwar period. The restreamlining was undertaken by National Railway Museum in York, Tyseley Locomotive Works at Birmingham Railway Museum the 229 club and magazine Steam Railway, whose readers donated £35,000.

Andrew Scott, NRM director, says: "This project was the impossible dream for many

Above: Bob Meanley who led the restreamlining team

years. It recreates one of the most significant products of the streamlined era.

"The engineering team were terrific. Apart from the steel problem, remaking the engine's front casing doors was a nightmare, as they're two hinged quarter-spheres.

Bob Meanley adds: "There was no detailed drawings for the front doors, so we had to work from enlarged photographs.

STREAMLINED TRAVEL IN 1937

It was 71 years ago, but Jean Shuttleworth (left), now 88, has never forgotten her journey on the brand new Coronation Scot express.

Aged 17, Mrs Shuttleworth made her first unaccompanied journey from Portsmouth, joining the streamlined train from London for Scotland in August 1937.

"I was visiting my aunt and family in Ayrshire and then we went to the Highlands. The journey took six and a half hours to Glasgow," says Mrs Shuttleworth, who lives in Derbyshire.

"The train was blue with silver stripes along it. The food was lovely and cost two shillings. It was cooked onboard and not wrapped in cellophane like today.

"It was the beginning of the grouse shooting season and there were lots of dogs all over the train. They weren't made to stay in the guard's van.

"I'm told it was luxurious, but at 17 you don't think about these things!"

PETE'S STEAM DREAM ACADEMY

POP MUSIC GIVES RECORD PRODUCER
PETE WATERMAN THE WHEREWITHAL TO
RESTORE BRITAIN'S RAILWAY HERITAGE

Pop music mogul and Britain's most famous "rail-nut" Pete Waterman puts his considerable money where his mouth is to keep steam trains running.

The cash for his expensive rail passion comes from scoring 22 British number one singles with his various acts and more than £500m of worldwide sales.

The Liverpool Daily Post & Echo's Live Steam from Lime Street programme will be a major beneficiary of his expert team at LNWR Heritage railway works.

His 21 full-time staff members in Crewe are busy restoring the world-famous No 6100 Royal Scot to mainline standard, aiming for a debut on our trains in August.

Further excitement is caused by LNWR Heritage restoring British Railways' former flagship locomotive No 70000 Britannia, owned by financier Jeremy Hosking, available later this year, or early in 2010.

"Britannia is fantastic and we've finished its brand new firebox and boiler, built in the traditional way. You'll be amazed when you see it," says Pete.

Additionally, LNWR Heritage retubed and overhauled No 6201 Princess Elizabeth at Crewe, its new home shed, after moving from Bury, on the East Lancs Railway.

Although Pete's LNWR Crewe maintenance company was sold to Arriva Trains in November 2008, he remains as chairman of LNWR Heritage.

"I've kept the engineering bit that I like, which does the serious welding, bending and cutting, In a locomotive works you've got welders, machinists, electricians, fitters, woodworkers – that's what it takes to keep a steam engine going. It's unbelievable, we've even got chimney sweeps. It's like a mini-world in itself. At its peak, 15,000 people were employed at Crewe railway works.

"They made everything, including gas and glass, except for their own toilet paper, as Izal had the toilet rights to supply all British railway trains. We won the war on the skills that the railways built up. Ironically, the only people putting money into Crewe at the moment is the German-owned Bentley car company. The Germans look at the downturn differently. They're training up people while everyone else in Britain is shedding them."

All of Pete's staff have served time with the company as apprentices and three apprenticeships are offered every year. The original staff are now retired, but are termed "buddies" and return to mentor the apprentices. In five years time every member of his 21 staff will be time-served.

"Britain is the king of these skills, but I'm not waving the banner just for the sake of it as this is what we need to keep going. There are no short cuts. You can't take a kid off the street and ask him to fix a steam engine the next day. He needs two or three years training before letting loose on one." says Pete.

Above:
Pete Waterman
with Britainnia

Below:
Britainnia's official
BR portrait after
completion at
Crewe in 1951

Opposite Page:
Pete Waterman at
Britainnia's
controls at Crewe
Heritage Centre

GREAT SCOT

BUILT IN 1930 AT DERBY, DESIGNED BY SIR HENRY FOWLER, IT WAS ONE OF THE 70-STRONG ROYAL SCOT CLASS WHICH STEAMED ALONG THE LONDON MIDLAND AND SCOTTISH MAINLINES

THE LMS premier locomotive Royal Scot was once as famous as its LNER rival, Flying Scotsman. Both were built to haul their respective companies' most prestigious Anglo-Scottish expresses of the same names. Unlike Flying Scotsman's glittering high-profile preservation career, first with owner businessman Alan Pegler, who saved it from the scrapyard, and now with the National Railway Museum, Royal Scot had long disappeared from the public eye.>>>

>>> This was partly because Royal Scot was soon eclipsed by larger LMS engines, but also because Sir Billy Butlin (to whom we should be very grateful) preserved it as a static exhibit at his Skegness Holiday Camp.

Flying Scotsman has been almost continuously kept in mainline running order, whereas Royal Scot was stuffed and mounted. However, that is all to change. While Flying Scotsman undergoes an extremely lengthy and costly rebuild at York, Royal Scot will return to the mainline rails this summer for the first time in 47 years.

Designed by Sir Henry Fowler, Royal Scot was built in 1930 at Derby, one of the 70-strong Royal Scot class. This was a remarkably successful design, especially given it was conceived in haste to resolve a motive power crisis created by the LMS's then small-engine policy, which was unable to cope with growing demand for heavier and faster trains.

Royal Scot itself achieved a major coup in 1933 when invited to appear at the World Trade Exposition, in Chicago, USA. It also toured the US and Canada hauling trains before returning home, with a commemorative bell mounted on the front buffer beam.

Royal Scot
running-in after
47 trainless years, at
Llangollen Railway's
Steel Steam and
Stars Gala,
in April 2009
Picture:
Stephen Done

William Stanier's Princess Royal and then Princess Coronation classes took over the top-link expresses from 1933 onwards, but Royal Scot and its classmates remained stalwarts on fast and heavy passenger trains up until 1965 when replaced by diesels.

Postwar, the Royal Scots were greatly revitalised by Stanier's major rebuilding programme (Royal Scot being done in 1950). For decades the class were a familiar sight working out of Liverpool to London, Leeds, Glasgow and Holyhead.

Butlins sold Royal Scot to Bressingham Steam Museum, at Diss, Norfolk, which occasionally steamed it between 1972 and 1978 on a short line. When expensive repairs became necessary, it returned to being a static exhibit.

Then Bressingham embarked on an ambitious plan to return Royal Scot to mainline use. Longer and costlier than expected, the restoration is being done by Pete Waterman's LNWR Heritage works at Crewe.

The restoration will be paid for as Royal Scot earns money through being hired out - a generous and flexible move by Pete Waterman.>>>

Above: Royal Scot class No.46106 Gordon Highlander arrives in Crewe with The Manxman Express (Liverpool-London) in 1951

> "Royal Scot is one of the world's most famous locomotives and we've got to make it one of the best.

>>> "Well, it's a pragmatic approach. Not everyone would do it, but not everyone's a rail-nut," chortled Pete.

He won't say how much the restoration cost, yet adds cryptically: "It doesn't help the public to know, but enthusiasts realise it costs up to £1m to restore a steam loco.

"There's no point pushing how much it costs as it would never get done - or their wives might find out how much they're spending.

"Royal Scot's boiler is fine but we've had huge problems with its bottom end. This has been a massive job to finish it properly. We were shocked to find that more needs to be done than we were told initially.

"Our boys couldn't get the valve gear to balance because, along with lots of other pieces, it was far more badly worn than expected.

"We're having to put in new cylinder rings and liners. It's the equivalent of having a major problem with your car gearbox.

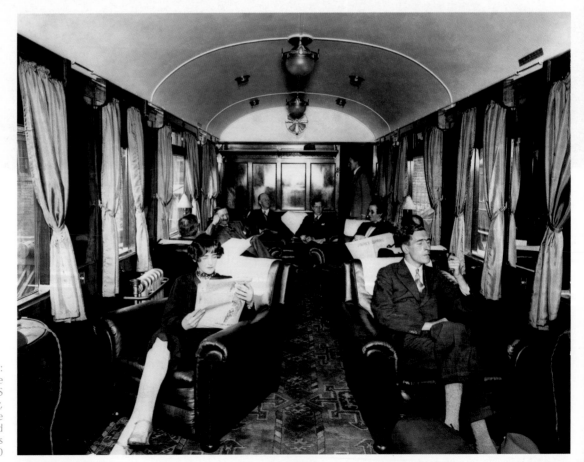

Right: The club-like interior of an LMS first class lounge car, introduced on the Merseyside and Royal Scot Expresses in 1930

Above:
The LNWR Heritage
engineering team
which restored
Royal Scot at
Crewe, in April,
2009

"Metals deteriorate all the time and I don't think that Royal Scot has had a major overhaul since 1955, which is 54 years ago."

Royal Scot's 1950 rebuilding with a modern boiler created a "practically a new loco," says Pete.

He adds: "We now treat locos with a lot of respect. Restoration has changed dramatically in the last 15 years and far more can be done than just a decade ago.

"In the latter years of steam these engines never had love lavished on them as we do. We don't patch up, but do proper repairs."

Royal Scot is only one of two survivors from its class, with No 46115 Scots Guardsman, based at Carnforth and restored for mainline use in 2008 by David Smith, West Coast Railway Company Chairman.

"Royal Scot is one of the world's most famous locomotives and we've got to make it one of the best. When Royal Scot comes to Liverpool I want to be on the footplate with my shovel working as a fireman."

ROYAL CLASS ACT OF THE RAILS

PRINCESS ELIZABETH - RECORD-BREAKER
WITH A TRACK RECORD TO MATCH HER NAMESAKE

Princess Elizabeth cruises over
Afon Cefni viaduct at Mallraeth
Anglesey, hauling the Queen's
80th anniversary special in April
2006. Picture: Eryl Crump

ONE of the all-time greats in the British locomotive pantheon, Princess Elizabeth is also the most famous locomotive to be based at Edge Hill shed, in Liverpool.

Second member of the Princess Royal class and built at Crewe in 1933, Lizzie was chosen to perform high speed London - Glasgow and return test runs in 1936 in preparation for introducing the streamlined Coronation Scot express service to rival the LNER's Coronation.

Lizzie performed so well that the Coronation Scot, hauled by the newer Princess Coronation class, never surpassed her speed record, which stands to this day. These exploits caused her Princess Royals classmates to be nicknamed Lizzies. >>>

Princess Elizabeth
brings The North
Wales Coast Express
into Frodsham,
Cheshire, for a
watering stop

>>> Designed by William Stanier, the 13-strong class were constructed to haul the famous Royal Scot express from London to Glasgow, taking over the accelerated service from the eponymous Royal Scot class itself.

Ousted themselves by the Princess Coronation class on Royal Scot express duties, the class became long-associated with the Liverpool Lime Street – London Euston top-link turns, such as The Merseyside Express and The Red Rose.

The Princess Royal class name was chosen as Mary, Princess Royal, was commander in chief of the Royal Scot regiment. Each class member was named after a princess, with No 6201 named after the Queen when a little girl. Interestingly, the other preserved survivor is Princess Margaret Rose, named after the Queen's late sister.

The class was withdrawn in the early 1960s as BR dieselisation marched on, but Lizzie was saved from the scrapyard thanks to a Cardiff dentist, Richard Bell and two friends.

Appalled that Lizzie was not considered worthy of preservation by officialdom, they raised the cash to buy the engine in 1962.

Each class member was named after a princess, with No 6201 named after the Queen when a little girl.

Above: Record-breaking LMS driver Tom Clark OBE and his fireman admire Meccano's new Hornby Princess Elizabeth model alongside the original at Edge Hill shed in 1937 (Picture Courtesy Micheal Foster/Hornby Hobbies)

Right: "Lizzie" stands over the ash-pit at Crewe's Great Gathering in September, 2005

6201

THE SOUTH AFRICAN CONNECTION

WITH THE GRACE OF A SPRINGBOK AND THE SPEED OF A CHEETAH, A4 CLASS UNION OF SOUTH AFRICA OUTPACES RIVALS

THERE is nothing on Britain's railways that looks anything remotely like the streamlined A4 class, regarded as LNER chief mechanical engineer Sir Nigel Gresley's masterpiece.

The unmistakable curvaceous bulk of the boiler, with its wedge-shaped "cod's mouth" snout, is said to be inspired by pre-war Bugatti racing cars.

This is complemented by the sensuous sheer of the footplate over the driving wheels, revised at the last minute to use the aerodynics of the R101 airship.

Far from being form without substance, these express locomotives, regarded as steam's last great pre-war fling before dieselisation, are compact, powerful and very fast.>>>

"No 9" Union of South Africa roars through the Highland snow with Railway Touring Company's Perth-bound Fair Maid.
Picture: Bob Green

Top: "No 9 streaks through Rainhill with Art in the Age of Steam excursion Scarborough-Liverpool in July 2008

Above: Driver Robert Morrison ready to leave Lime Street with inaugural North Wales Coast Express on August 8, 2008

Right: Entering Conwy

>>>Three of the remaining A4s hold records: our own No 60009 Union of South Africa achieved the fastest London – Edinburgh steam locomotive run; No 60007 Sir Nigel Gresley is holder of the official postwar steam speed record at 112mph and, of course, Mallard has the accolade of being the world's fastest steam locomotive achieving 126mph.

Built in 1937, Union of South Africa was one of a batch named after the British Empire's most important colonies and designated to haul the Coronation, a London – Edinburgh deluxe streamlined express.

The springbok plaque on the driver's side of the locomotive was donated in 1954 by a Bloemfontain newspaper proprietor. Even more distinctively, it is also fitted with a South African Railways-type chime whistle.

Above: The unmistakable bulk of A4 class
Union of South Africa crossses Church Street, Frodsham,
on The North Wales Express August 8, 2008

Right: Leaving Llandudno Junction

A Scottish-based locomotive throughout its
mainline life, Union of South Africa, nicknamed "No 9", was allocated to Edinburgh
from new and in 1962 was transferred to
Aberdeen.

It hauled the last booked steam hauled train
from Kings Cross in October 1964 and was
the last steam loco to be overhauled at
Doncaster whilst in service.

Purchased from British Railways by one of
Scotland's biggest farmers, John Cameron, in
July 1966, No 9 has accumulated the highest
mileage of any locomotive in the class. The
loco is now based at Thornton Junction, in

BLACK IS BACK AT LIME STREET

THAT MOST HANDSOME WORKHORSE OF THE RAILWAYS,
THE STANIER BLACK FIVE, STILL STEAMING ON AFTER 75 YEARS

NEVER has an example of a machine's beauty derived from function been so satisfyingly achieved as in the Stanier Black Five steam locomotives.

These handsome, perfectly-proportioned locomotives exude style and power, looking like the seminal mid-20th century steam engine.

Yet they were ostensibly unpretentious, mixed traffic, go-anywhere, do anything, maids of all work, built to plug the LMS's seemingly endless motive power crisis. Designed by William Stanier, obviously, for the LMS, this Class 5 4-6-0 type was painted black – hence its universal nickname.

The 842-strong class, built from 1934 to 1951, so far exceeded its design expectations that they were as happy hauling heavy expresses as pottering around with pick-up freights. >>>

Above: The second York Yuletide Express run on December 21 2008, with Driver Albert Seymour, owner of 45407, Ian Riley and waving off the train hairdresser Herbert-Howe

Liverpool Lord Mayor Cllr Steve Rotherham waves off the first York Yuletide Express at Liverpool Lime Street, on December 14, 2008

As the latterday backbone of North West England and North Wales railway motive power, the Black Fives served until the very last day of mainline steam on British Railways in 1968. During their heyday, they could be seen the length of Britain, from Wick and Thurso on the northern Scottish coast to Bournemouth, on the English south coast.

Eighteen Black Fives are preserved, including No 45407, The Lancashire Fusilier, used for the Liverpool Daily Post & Echo's Live Steam from Lime Street season. This was one of the huge batch of 227 ordered from Armstrong-Whitworth, Newcastle upon Tyne, in 1936. The bulk of the class were built at Crewe and Derby, with 80 constructed at Vulcan Foundry, Newton-le-Willows.

No 45407 was one of the final Black 5s withdrawn on August 4, 1968. It was saved by the late Dr Peter Beet (whose son owns LMS Jubilee Class 5690 Leander) and millionaire David Davis.

After residing at Carnforth's Steamtown centre, it is now owned by leading steam railway engineer Ian Riley. He named it The Lancashire Fusilier, in honour of Bury's own regiment, where the loco engine is based at Riley & Son's works, on the East Lancashire Railway.

Ian regards No 45407 as one of the best of an outstanding class and it certainly proved its mettle, effortlessly hauling the LDPE's two York Yuletide Expresses last Christmas, as a last-minute stand-in for the more powerful Duke of Gloucester and Leander, which had both become unavailable.

Opposite page: DriverBill Andrews places a holly wreath appropriately from Rainhill Florists, on the first Yuletide Express Pictures: Tracey O'Neill

FROM GREY LADY TO GREEN GODDESS

BRITAINS BIGGEST NEW-BUILD HERITAGE LOCOMOTIVE PROJECT HAS BLOWN AWAY THE CRITICS AS TORNADO TAKES TO THE RAILS

Top: HRH Prince Charles, Prince of Wales at the Tornado's naming ceremony

Above: Mark Allatt A1 Steam Locomotive Trust's chairman giving his speech at the ceremony in August 2008

It was a vision that few dared contemplate and which has taken two decades of unremitting hard work to reach a triumphant conclusion.

This was the project to build the first mainline steam locomotive in Britain in nearly 40 years. The £3m result, No 60103 Tornado, has far exceeded expectations since first moving in steam in August, 2008.

And we hope that this sensational latest chapter in British railway achievement will join the Liverpool Daily Post & Echo's Live Steam from Lime Street roster before the year's end.

Tornado is a London North Eastern Railway A1 class express passenger locomotive designed in 1947 by its chief mechanical engineer, Arthur Peppercorn, in Doncaster for East Coast Mainline duties.

Astonishly, by 1966, all of the 49 A1 class locomotives were scrapped due to rapid dieselisation, so a group of rail enthusiasts decided one evening in a pub to build one. As you do.

The sensational outcome is one that encapsulates, as the Prince of Wales said at

Tornado's naming ceremony in York last February, the best of British, in skill, craftsmanship, ingenuity, individuality and sheer determination against tremendous odds.

Conceived and built by the A1 Steam Locomotive Trust, this Darlington-based charity was formed in 1990 to complete the next logical, but untested stage of the locomotive heritage movement, building a brand new steam locomotive.

In building a steam locomotive for the 21st century railway, not only has the Trust had to incorporate modern safety electronics, but also devise innovative funding through convenants and bonds, plus commercial sponsorship.

Mark Allatt, Trust chairman, says: "In contrast to various other heritage projects, we treated funding as a priority and not a distraction.

"We also wanted to use professionals in their fields for the various posts needed and to use the engineering industry for all manufacturing to meet railway certification."

By October 1999, the trust had more supporters than any UK locomotive owning group. It has raised record-breaking amounts by rail fans through covenanting, but still has to service debts of more than £800,000.>>>

Top: Tornado's wheels the LNER teak coach set along the North Yorkshire Moors Railway

Above: Two generations admire Britain's latest mainline steam loco

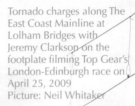

Tornado charges along The East Coast Mainline at Lolham Bridges with Jeremy Clarkson on the footplate filming Top Gear's London-Edinburgh race on April 25, 2009
Picture: Neil Whitaker

Top: The boiler is fitted to Tornado, the first steam locomotive built in Britain for more than 50 years

Middle: Mark Allatt, A1 Steam Locomotive Trust's chairman with Trust president Dorothy Mather, widow of designer Arthur Peppercorn

Bottom: Tornado on a trial run in its grey undercoat on the Great Central Railway

>>>Tornado is built from scratch, with no recovered or restored parts, a feat never achieved in the UK railway preservation before, although its cost has doubled.

The Trust's president is Dorothy Mather, widow of the A1 designer Arthur Peppercorn, and the vice president is Peter Townend, former London King's Cross shed manager, who daily dealt with A1 class members.

TORNADO will be back in the news again at the time of our planned Liverpool trains, with the June broadcast of BBC Two's Top Gear.

This will feature a 400-mile race between the A1 class steam locomotive, a vintage motorbike and a classic sports car. The highly popular programme's aim is to recreate the Races to the North atmosphere, so beloved of Victorian railway companies and last staged by the London North Eastern Railway with Flying Scotsman in the 1930s. Chief presenter Jeremy Clarkson apparently pulled rank over co-presenter Richard "Hamster" Hammond to travel on Tornado's footplate from London King's Cross to Edinburgh Waverley station.

"Clarkson comes from Doncaster, so we assume deep down he has a fond allegiance to LNER pacific locos like Tornado," says Mark Allatt, chairman of the A1 Locomotive Trust.

Instead, Hammond rode a Vincent Black Shadow motorbike and his fellow presenter, James May (who is a rail buff), drove a Jaguar XK120.

The outcome is a closely guarded secret, but we believe that Tornado acquitted herself exceptionally well.

Mrs Mather lit the first fire in Tornado's firebox and rode on the footplate for the inaugural run at Darlington works and says: "My husband would be so proud and would have wanted to be here so much."

Mark Allatt says: "We're all absolutely delighted with Tornado's outstanding performance to-date. It's felt like a miracle made possible by our 2,000 donors, sponsors, volunteers and contractors.

"Tornado will almost certainly become as legendary as Flying Scotsman and Mallard, two of the original A1 class' east coast stable-mates. Doubtless this locomotive too will bring fascination and pleasure to millions."

The A1 Locomotive Trust needs further help from volunteers and donors to keep Tornado running, Tel: 01325 460163, or email www.a1steam.com

BUTLIN RED COATED EXPRESS

THE CRIMSON DUCHESS IS BACK IN HER LIVERPOOL HOME FOR ONE MORE SEASON

S HE'S the mighty aristocrat of the mainline and needs one driver, two firemen and three fitters to keep her running at full-power.

This is Princess Coronation class No 6233 Duchess of Sutherland, Britain's most powerful express steam locomotive and a former denizen of Edge Hill depot for hauling top-link

Completed in July 1938 at Crewe at a cost of £13,000, the Duchess and her classmates were William Stanier's tour de force, representing the zenith of London Midland & Scottish steam power.

It appears that 2009 will be the Duchess' last mainline season as she is due for a major overhaul, at a price far in excess of her

>>>Both Duchess of Sutherland and classmate Duchess of Hamilton were withdrawn from Edge Hill in early 1964, but thankfully saved from the scrapyard by Sir Billy Butlin, who bought them directly from the shed.

Hamilton was put on static display at Butlins Camp in Minehead and Sutherland went to Butlins Camp at Heads of Ayr, in Scotland.

Later moved to Bressingham Steam Museum in Norfolk, Duchess of Sutherland was eventually purchased by The Princess Royal Class Locomotive Trust and restored at its Midland Railway Butterley base for mainline operation.

While presented in authentic 1946 exterior condition, beneath the Duchess' gleaming crimson-lake livery are all the high-tech gizmos needed for running on railways in 2009.

These are TPWS (Train Protection & Warning System), OTMR (On-train Monitoring and Recording equipment) and Automatic Warning System (AWS). In addition to her original vacuum brakes, she has the contemporary air-brake system.

Malcolm Baker, Trust chairman and an IT engineer, who has been involved with the locomotive since 1996, says: "There's a lot of dirty unglamorous work needed to keep her going.

"For a Saturday job we'd light the fire around 4pm the day before. She simmers overnight with steam at about 100psi, then first thing in the morning we raise the steam pressure, oil up at 7.30am and would be ready for the off at 9am.

"But it's all worthwhile to be on the footplate when she's working hard at 75mph with a 13-coach train. You can really feel her stretching her muscles as she eats up the miles."

The Duchess was the first steam locomotive to haul the Royal Train for 39 years, carrying the Queen and Prince Philip from Holyhead to Llandudno Junction, on June 11, 2002, during their Golden Jubilee tour of North Wales.

"But it's all worthwhile to be on the footplate when she's working hard at 75mph with a 13-coach train. You can really feel her stretching her muscles as she eats up the miles."

By strange chance, the locomotive had been on stand-by for British Railways' final steam hauled Royal Train in 1963. Serendipitously, the 2002 journey also coincided with the 160th anniversary of the first Royal train in 1842.

A second Royal Train duty occurred on March 22, 2005, when the Duchess took the Prince of Wales from Settle to Carlisle, for the 25th anniversary of Friends of the Settle & Carlisle, which helped save the line.

Above: Brell Ewart - ex-chairman of the Princess Royal Class Locomotive Trust presents HRH the Queen with a special commemorative headlamp at Llandudno Junction station 11 June 2002

Top: The Duchess of Sutherland steams through Penmaenmawr hauling the Royal Train

TAKING A STEP BACK IN TIME AND MOTION

CLASSIC STEAM TRAIN TOURS OF A BYGONE AGE FROM LIME STREET, LIVERPOOL

We are tempting our passengers with more variety in this second year of the Liverpool Daily Post & Echo's Live Steam from Lime Street season, in association with the Railway Touring Company.

For the first time we will offer Premier Class silver service dining on the North Wales Coast Express. Also the train will detour for those wishing to visit Llandudno town itself.

After the success of The Barbie Shop trio singing onboard last year's York Yuletide Expresses, we plan to have more performers entertaining passengers onboard. The York Yuletide Express will run again on December 13.

Our rolling stock features The Royal Scot rake of coaches built c1960 - c1970, fully-refurbished by owners Railway Touring Co and Riviera Trains.

With their fine wooden panelling and a spaciousness unknown on modern passenger stock, these coaches evoke the glamorous age of express steam train travel in the postwar period.

Nigel Dobbing, managing director of Railway Touring Company, says: "We're delighted to help bring steam trains back to Liverpool. The response has been overwhelming, especially as we were not sure how last year's first season would be greeted. The other surprise was the popularity of Premier Dining Class. We had to put extra coaches on to cope with demand."

All of our trains include three classes of travel:
■ Premier Dining includes full English breakfast, and four course dinner silver served at your seat in Pullman-style. Longer journeys include light lunch.
■ First Class includes morning coffee and Danish pastries and tea and biscuits in the afternoon.
■ Standard Class includes a reserved seat at a table for four.

Additionally, a buffet car is available and serves tea, coffee, snacks and light refreshments.

Tables for two can be guaranteed in first class and premier dining for a supplement of £15 per person, subject to availability.

THE COAST TO COAST EXPRESS – SATURDAY JULY 4, 2009

The Coast to Coast Express will run from Liverpool to Scarborough, linking the Irish Sea with the North Sea, hauled by No 6201 Princess Elizabeth.

Steaming out of Liverpool Lime Street, the train heads east along the old Liverpool & Manchester Railway. After picking up more passengers at Rainhill ,St Helens Junction and Manchester Victoria, we continue through Stalybridge with its famous buffet, on the climb over the Pennines and through Standedge Tunnel - one of the longest in the UK.

After the final passenger boarding in Huddersfield, we take the old Lancashire and Yorkshire Railway to Wakefield Kirkgate. Heading through Castleford, our locomotive takes water at York where passengers may leave the train for the afternoon or continue to Scarborough.

York has many attractions, including the Minster, The Shambles, Jorvik Viking Centre and the matchless National Railway Museum. Open-topped buses leave from York Railway Station for city tours.

On leaving York, the Scarborough line crosses the River Ouse and allows a fast run along the Vale of York before slowing for the curves to follow the river past Kirkham Abbey. Soon we pass through Malton and Seamer to arrive at Scarborough.

Scarborough claims to be Britain's original seaside resort and the premier one of East Coast resort.

APPROXIMATE TIMINGS:

Station	Depart	Return
Liverpool Lime Street	07:50	21:00
Rainhill	08:05	20:45
St Helens Junction	08:15	20:35
Manchester Victoria	08:45	19:55
Huddersfield	09:20	19:15
York	11:00	17:40
Scarborough	Arrive 12:00	Depart 16:40

FARES:

Fare	Adult	Junior	Family
Premier	£169	£120	£499
First	£89	£49	£289
Standard	£66	£35	£199

for £5 discount per passenger quote code CCE

THE CUMBRIAN MOUNTAIN EXPRESS - SATURDAYS, AUGUST 1 AND 22

The Cumbrian Mountain Express departs from Liverpool Lime Street to pick up more passengers at St Helens, joining the West Coast Main Line with further stops at Wigan and Preston.

A fast run along the West Coast Main Line will take us to Carnforth for the engine to be watered. We will ascend the first severe gradient up to Grayrigg, then steam through the beautiful Lune Valley gaining speed for the ascent of Shap.

After crossing the Cumbrian Fells, we descend to Penrith and head onwards to the border city of Carlisle. We stay in Carlisle for almost three hours, giving ample opportunity to explore the castle, cathedral and shops.

Soon after leaving the city, the climb starts on the Settle & Carlisle Railway and back over the Pennines. More water stop is taken at Appleby, then onwards to England's highest railway summit, Ais Gill, at 1,169 feet.

We cross magnificent viaducts, such as Ribblehead, and through long tunnels against the backdrop of Penyghent, Whernside and Ingleborough mountains.

A fast run down through Settle brings the train to Long Preston, stopping at Wigan (passengers for Preston alight here), St Helens and Lime Street, arriving before 8pm.

APPROXIMATE TIMINGS:

Station	Depart	Return
Liverpool Lime St.	08:35	19:45
St. Helens Central	08:55	19:20
Wigan Nth. Western	09:10	19:00
Preston	09:30	———
Carlisle	Arrive 11:45	Depart 14:30

FARES

Fares	Adult	Junior	Family
Premier	£179	£112	£475
First	£109	£55	£295
Standard	£74	£39	£195

for £5 discount per passenger quote code CME

THE NORTH WALES COAST EXPRESS - SUNDAYS AUGUST 2, 9, 16, 23 & 30

The North Wales Coast Express will run five times this August - twice more than last year. The trains will be hauled again by our stalwarts Princess Elizabeth and Union of South Africa, but joined by newcomers Duchess of Sutherland and, making its first mainline debut in 47 years, Royal Scot.

Also new this year is the addition of Premier Dining onboard the train and a Llandudno stop.

In a highly atmospheric departure from Lime Street, our train will storm up through the deep cutting to Edge Hill, stopping to pick up passengers at Broad Green station (which has a large car park), before calling at Warrington Bank Quay, Frodsham and Chester.

The exit from Chester is through the Roman walls, across the River Dee and into Wales, running alongside the Dee Estuary and the Irish Sea.

Passing Prestatyn and Rhyl, the North Wales Mainline hugs this delightful coastline, renowned for its beaches. Our first stop is Colwyn Bay with its views of the Great Orme. For the first time in over a decade steam will return to Llandudno itself as the train will trasverse the branchline there in both directions so passengers can visit 'the Queen of North Wales resorts".

For those staying onboard, the train departs after the locomotive has taken water and crosses Conwy causeway and Stephenson's tubular Conwy Harbour Bridge, past the famous castle. The line runs very close to the sea, the train racing through little seaside resorts like Penmaenmawr and Llanfairfechan before arriving in Bangor. Passengers can leave at Bangor to explore this

fine university town with its pier or visit nearby mighty Penrhyn Castle.

Meantime, the train steams on to Anglesey, through more delightful coastal scenery, before terminating at Holyhead.

Our train departs Holyhead at around 16:30, stopping to collect passengers along the North Wales coast. It sets down passengers at Chester, Frodsham, Warrington Bank Quay and Broad Green, before finally steaming into Liverpool Lime Street.

Approximate Timings:

Station	Depart	Return
Liverpool Lime Street	10:05	20:00
Broad Green	10:23	19:50
Warrington Bank Quay	10:45	19:25
Frodsham	10:52	19:15
Chester	11:10	19:00
Colwyn Bay	12:05	18:10
Llandudno	12:15	18:00
Bangor	13:15	16:55
Holyhead	Arrive 13:40	Depart 16:30

Fares
Liverpool, Warrington and Chester to
Bangor and Holyhead

	Adult	Junior	Family
First	£89	£47	£239
Standard	£63	£35	£165

Liverpool, Warrington and Chester to
Colwyn Bay and Llandudno Junction

	Adult	Junior	Family
First	£79	£42	£210
Standard	£53	£29	£144

for £5 discount per passenger quote code NWC

GREAT JOURNEYS • FASCINATING PLACES
THE RAILWAY TOURING Co

For more information
Tel: 01553 661500 or
www.railwaytouring.co.uk

THE BOYS WITH THE BLACK STUFF

OLD STEAM TRAIN DRIVERS DON'T FADE AWAY THEY JUST KEEP ROLLING ON

BETWEEN them, they reckon to have clocked up 594 years' service, driving trains over millions of miles and carrying millions of passengers safely to their destinations.

And that's not even counting Sundays. These grand old men were public servants in the truest sense, often going beyond the call of duty, and as they said: "We did not work for the railways, we got paid by them."

They are the retired drivers of Garston's British Railways Club, who, weary of supping pints (well, not entirely weary) at their Thursday afternoon get-togethers, decided to turn back the clock and try their hand on a real steam train once more.

Organised by former colleague Trevor Gargan an irrepressible character (actually, they're all irrepressible), they sally forth in a minibus to revive their skills on preserved lines like the Welsh Highland Railway or East Lancashire Railway.

I caught up with them at the Llangollen Steam Railway, by the foaming River Dee, where waits the simmering, dark green Manor class locomotive No 7822, Foxcote Manor, all polished brass and copper trim.

Foxcote Manor is a Great Western Railway locomotive design, an important fact, as most of our doughty footplate crew are either ex-London Midland & Scottish or London North Eastern Railway and their equivalent British Railways regional successors.

Like tribal allegiances, even in old age these loyalties cannot be broken. Inspecting the spartan working conditions, Dougie Carver, ex-Great Western Railway, said: "You got a proper seat on the LNER.

"Whereas Sir Felix Pole, the GWR's general manager, decreed 'We do not pay men to sit down'. Eventually the GWR gave us a piece of wood to sit on, so we were lucky."

Spencer Wissett, 74, worked for 44 years on the railways, starting in 1953 at Brunswick shed, before working at Walton, Edge Hill, Garston and Warrington.

He said: "All of us here have got steam in the blood, but I needed a few tips when I was on the engine. Mind you, this engine is a right hand drive 'Wezzy' one, whereas we're London Midland Region and had much better engines. We had smaller shovels then the GW, as befits men who are more skilful!"

With his walking stick and exuding presence, Pat Mitchell seems like a brigadier inspecting his troops and pronounces: "Isambard Kingdom Brunel was a waste of space with the GWR. He should have stuck to building ships and bridges."

Pat has a row of badges down his lapel. "That's my veterans' badge," he said and somebody behind sniggers, "Yeah, for being in the Boy Scouts!"

Unabashed, he continues: "No, it commemorates 40 years being exploited by Aslef." He also has a badge, in case we hadn't realised, with the words "I am the driver" donated by a young relative >>>

Top: Event organiser and former driver Trevor Gargan

Opposite page: Crewe driver Bob Hart sports some natty headgear- a J-cloth to keep the cinders and smuts out of his hair. Picture: Stephen Done

>>> A couple of the gang board the footplate to drive and everybody else piles into the train awaiting their turn.

The locomotive's regulator (ie, accelerator) is crisp and needs a delicate touch. With a sudden loud woofing sound, the loco's wheels slip and a cheer goes up from our drivers. "He's a bit to eager to get away," they chortle.

"Get out and pump up the tyres," someone chirps, to much laughter. To louder guffaws someone yells: "Get out and milk it."

All agree that, although the hours were bad, the railways' working conditions were good and the camaraderie was terrific, but Christmas and Boxing Days were awkward for families.

Pat Mitchell (above) waves his stick at the benign form of Harry Grieves and says: "Fifty years ago, that man abused me."

Raising an eyebrow, Harry whispers: "But not in the way you think."

Pat adds: "I fired for him on Christmas Day on the 5.05, all stations Liverpool to Stockport, and we carried three passengers. There were 24 stations, including three in Widnes."

"Hmm. I only remember stopping at 21," muses Harry.

Trevor Gargan, from Aigburth, organised this particular day out with Barry Allen. Trevor says: "I started in Brunswick in 1959 then moved to Garston where I was made a driver.

"It was like a holiday camp at Speke shed, even though you'd jobs like having to clean the engines' fires out at night. Everyone got on.

"Ray Gosling was my first fireman and it's hard to believe that he's now retired. Harry Grieves has had two artificial legs, but was determined to come today. As a driver, he'd always help you out with firing and let you drive. He's one of the best."

Barry Allen joined the railways in 1962, at Widnes North, on the old Cheshire Lines Committee's Liverpool - Manchester route.

The family supplied at least six drivers to the famous CLC. In earlier times, railway services like the CLC were dominated by certain families, such as the Cooks and Marriotts.

"The big difference between today and years ago is that trains back then were not so crowded as they were much longer – eight or 10 coaches."

STEAM SPEED DEMONS

A SEEMINGLY unassuming man, John Anthony, 70, of St Helens, holds a great distinction in railway annals.

He was the last man to drive the world's fastest steam locomotive, Mallard, now incarcerated in the National Railway Museum, York.

After working for 15 years as a driver at Garston shed, he transferred to Skipton which supplied drivers for the historic and scenic Settle & Carlisle Railway.

"Drivers volunteered for the Settle & Carlisle steam charters," says John. "I was the last person to drive Mallard on a passenger train in 1986, on the 50th anniversary of the speed record."

One of British Railways' last drivers "passed out" (certified) to drive steam locos, initially he was employed driving heavy freights such as the Ford Halewood car trains from Ditton to Rugby.

"Garston shed was very relaxed compared to the atmosphere at Skipton. At Garston we'd be going all over the place – Manchester Exchange, Llandudno, Blackpool.

"Very soon we were transferred to diesel electric locos which were wonderful. Steam engines are dirty and hard work."

Tales abound about their colleagues' eccentricities, such as the guard who had a phobia about tunnels, or the Garston loco lamp collector, always smartly dressed with a dicky-bow tie.

The post-war speed record for a steam locomotive is officially 112mph, but Spencer Wissett (below) claims he went faster through Ditton Junction, as fireman on a night-time mail train.

"We were coming back from Crewe to Liverpool on the 1.45am postal train, which had just two coaches on," says Spencer, 73, of Netherley.

"After coming through Runcorn and crossing the bridge, my driver Charles Ebsworth said 'Let's see how she goes', as it was a clear, straight line from Ditton Junction.

"The engine was Princess Helena Victoria, one of the Princess Royal class which were very powerful and based at Edge Hill for the heavy Liverpool - London expresses.

"He pulled the regulator down and she raced away, the speedo shot up to 115mph. She was rolling a bit, but otherwise very steady. You didn't feel in danger.

"By then it was about 2.20am and there was nobody to see it. I didn't think of it as an achievement. It just happened, part of the fun of the job."

STRICTLY COME STEAMING

ARMY-STYLE discipline was the norm if you worked for the Great Western Railway and its successor British Railways Western Region, recalls Douglas Carver, 72, of Penketh.

"I started work on the railways, aged 15, as an engine cleaner, the traditional way of becoming a driver. Although a fireman from age of 16, I was too young to work at night.

"The GWR was very strict and run like the military. If you were 10 minutes late on a 3am shift you'd be sent home and lose a day's pay, yet your shift could be moved by two hours either way.

"Lads today would not go through with it. But back then it was not a job, but a way of life. You had to get to your destination, the train must always go.

"If a component fails on a diesel or electric loco, you can't move. But on a steam loco you could take a hammer to it and get going again!"

These trains carried bullion and were met at Lime Street by three Post Office vans. One carried the bullion and the other two were decoys. All three converged on the main Post Office in Victoria Street.

"Back then, the footplate crews would have their favourite pubs and drink a few pints before setting off again. That wouldn't happen today!"

Spencer also recalls firing the mighty Duchess of Hamilton, based at Edge Hill shed, on a Liverpool London express in 1964.

"Electrification was already under way and there were no water troughs for the engine to pick up. It was a heavy train and was touch and go whether we'd make it to Crewe before we ran out of water.

"We made it and arrived in Euston about 30 minutes late, which was about average for that time."

Rails to North Wales and Beyond

The Chester and Holyhead Railway richly combines coast and castles

Conwy Castle and Jubilee class No 5690 Leander en route from Crewe to Holyhead having just taken on water at Llandudno Junction in September, 2005

Such was the speed of technological progress in the 19th century, that the great Victorian engineers and architects felt obliged to root their audacious advancements in the clothes of the past.

The industrial age sought a direct continuity with the agrarian world by cloaking their achievements in a style that was deliberately skewed to backwards, not forwards.

Engineer Robert Stephenson gave an Egyptian look to his pioneering Menai Bridge and Bangor's Belmont Tunnel portals on the Chester & Holyhead Railway.

It was as if to say, this is how Rameses II would have built it, had he been connecting the Upper Nile with Anglesey, on what is now known as the North Wales Coast Mainline. >>>

Above: Riddles Standard class 8P pacific No.71000 Duke of Gloucester accelerates out of Llandudno Junction for Holyhead

Below: Stanier Black Five crosses the Britannia Bridge with the Irish Mail 150th anniversary special in 1998

>>> In essence, a spur of the West Coast Main Line, the North Wales Coast Mainline was born of the Admiralty's decision to route the Irish Mail service from London via Holyhead to Dublin (being the shortest sea-route via Kingstown, now Dun Laoghaire).

This followed the 1801 Act of Union, integrating Ireland into the United Kingdom. The great engineer Thomas Telford was commissioned to upgrade the London – Holyhead road (the A5). He took his route through mountainous Snowdonia, via Llangollen and Betws-y-Coed, creating his magnificent suspension bridges at Menai Bridge and Conwy.

The Irish Mail, Britain's oldest and most venerable named express train service, was launched from London Euston to Holyhead on August 1, 1848, the same day as Chester General station was opened.

As "railway mania" was spreading, Robert Stephenson's famous father George was consulted on an Irish Mail route and predicted that fast and heavy trains would struggle through Snowdonia so he chose a northerly coastal route from Chester.

The first section from Crewe to Chester was built by the Chester & Crewe Railway and absorbed by the Grand Junction Railway (successor to the L&MR) shortly before opening in 1840.

After a fall-out with George Stephenson, the Chester & Holyhead board gave the engineering contract to Thomas Brassey, in partnership with William McKenzie Ross and Robert Stephenson.

The first sod was cut and the first blasting shot fired at Conwy tunnel on St David's Day, March 1, 1845. By year end, around some 5,000 men and 500 horses were building the line.

Work also started on Llandegai, Conwy, Belmont, Bangor and Penmaenbach tunnels. In spite of the route's flat profile there were considerable engineering problems. In October 1846, the sea defences were breached at Penmaenmawr tunnel entrances and the formation washed away before completion.

Stephenson, aided by William Fairbairn, was much occupied with two truly advanced structures – the River Conwy Tubular Bridge and the stupendous Britannia Tubular Bridge, over the Menai Strait.

However, the far less complex River Dee bridge at Chester almost ruined Stephenson's reputation. Opened in November 1846 for shared use with the Shrewsbury & Chester Railway (later GWR), one of its three 98 foot cast iron spans collapsed on May 24, 1847 just as a passenger train was crossing. The fireman and four passengers were killed and eight injured.

As a result, cast iron beam bridges reinforced by wrought iron tie bars were abandoned.

The Britannia Bridge was the final part to be finished of the Chester – North Wales coast section. Prior to completion, passengers had to switch to a stagecoach to cross Telford's road bridge and reboard another train at Llanfair PG.

The Irish Mail, Britain's oldest and most venerable named express train service, was launched from London Euston to Holyhead on August 1, 1848, the same day as Chester General station was opened.

Irish and North Wales passenger, mail and freight traffic was so heavy through the 19th and early 20th centuries that the world's first water troughs were installed at Mochdre.

Located between Colwyn Bay and Llandudno Junction, steam locomotives could lower scoops and replenish their water without stopping. Oh, that these were still available for preserved steam locos today.

Much of the line between Chester and Colwyn Bay was quadrupled to increase capacity, but these sections are now once again two tracks.

Left: Duchess of Sutherland, thunders through Penmaenmawr station in pouring rain.

CHESTER STATION

The designer of Chester General station, Francis Thompson, a celebrated local architect, chose an Italian palazzo style.

Approaching General station along the newly-built City Road, travellers were put in mind of a great southern European palace, rather than a mere mundane temple of steam.

Thompson's Italianate style became the hallmark of several stations along the North Wales Coast Mainline, which survive today.

Chester's importance as a railway and the machinations of LNWR's Machiavellian general manager Capt Mark Huish seemed to be working undisturbed, until the GWR snapped up the Shrewsbury & Chester Railway and arrived via the back-door.

To the LNWR's chagrin, it was forced into a joint-operation of the Chester – Birkenhead mainline, giving the GWR access to Merseyside's thriving dock traffic.

The GWR also introduced expresses between its London Paddington HQ and its fine terminus at Birkenhead Woodside.

This gave Chester General the kudos of being one of only three British stations in which London bound trains departed in opposite directions.

Chester railway station still retains its Italianate design by Francis Thompson

Capital-bound passengers could board westbound GWR expresses which reversed at Chester for Paddington, or LNWR eastbound expresses from North Wales for Euston.

This choice lasted well into BR days, until 1967 when the West Coast Mainline electrification from Crewe to Euston was completed and it became the preferred trunk route.

The GWR mainline with its hourly Birkenhead – Paddington expresses (running via Chester, Wrexham, Ruabon, Gobowen and Shrewsbury) was downgraded to a secondary route with two-hourly stopping services terminating at Birmingham.

Below: Ian Riley's Standard class 4 No 76079 at Chester station on a Cheshire Lines Special

Duchess of Sutherland on the way to Holyhead speeds into the eastbound portal of Llandegai tunnel, at Bangor. Pictures by Gwyn Roberts.

Above: Princess Elizabeth gets underway after a signal check at Penmaenmawr station

Left: Driver Bill Andrews leans out of Duchess of Sutherland's cab at Chester

Princess Elizabeth heads
northwards along the Settle
and Carlisle Railway.
Picture: Bob Green

YOU TAKE THE HIGH RAILROAD

THE SETTLE AND CARLISLE RAILWAY'S ROUTE ALONG THE ROOF-TOP OF ENGLAND GIVES MATCHLESS VIEWS.

THE highest mainline in Britain, the Settle & Carlisle Line has been dubbed "the Jane Russell of railways," as it shares the golden age Hollywood star's exciting curves and dizzying gradients.

The 73-mile long S&C is regarded as England's most scenic railway, running through mountain ranges which called for major engineering with numerous viaducts, tunnels, bridges, embankments and cuttings.

This is a remote windswept, weather-beaten area of the Yorkshire Dales and North Pennines. The S&C's conception, construction and survival have given it legendary status in railway annals. It is justifiably hailed as one of the jewels in the crown of Victorian enterprise and engineering.

It was the outcome of bloody-minded determination by the mighty Midland Railway, which was denied access to Scotland over the metals of the equally potent London & North Western Railway.>>>

>>>The Midland's directors could see only one solution – build their own tracks from Settle, up over the Pennines "the rooftop of England," to the great railway centre of Carlisle, where they could link up with other Scottish companies and by-pass the pugnacious LNWR.

Surveying began in 1865 and parliamentary approval granted a year later. But – guess what – a banking failure sparked a UK financial crisis. Interest rates shot up, some railways went bust and the Midland's board, scared by a shareholders' revolt reassessed the £2.3m project. Attempts to cancel the scheme it had previously fought for were refused by parliament and construction began in November, 1865.

Wth mechanical diggers yet to be invented, the line was built by more than 6,000 navvies, who toiled in some of England's vilest weather. Many of these labourers were Irish and vast camps were built to house them, which included post offices and schools.

Above:
A Stanier 8F class rolls off Ribblehead Viaduct with an excursion

Left:
Princess Elizabeth powers over the Pennines

The Midland Railway sponsored lay-preachers to try and moderate the navvies' drunken violence in these God-foresaken locations. These camps were given topical names such as Inkerman, Sebastapol and Jericho.

As befitted its concept, the S&C was engineered for long-distance express train running. Local traffic was an after-thought and many stations were miles from the villages whose names they display. Dent, at 1,110ft above sea-level, is four miles from the village. >>>

Opposite page:
An Atmospheric spring day as the Cumbrian Mountain Express as Duchess of Sutherland pounds up "The Long Drag"
Pictures: Stephen Done

Above:
Oliver Cromwell
heads north over
Ribblehead Viaduct
with the Fifteen
Guinea Special
re-enactment on
August 10, 2008

Unsurprisingly, footplate crews nicknamed this "The Long Drag."

The scheme still demanded 14 tunnels and 22 viaducts, with the most spectacular being the 24-arch Ribblehead Viaduct which is 104ft high and 440yds long. Its piers were sunk 25ft below the boggy peat surface and set in concrete to create stable foundations. Blea Moor Tunnel, 2,629yds long and 500ft beneath the fellsides, is sandwiched between Ribblehead and Dent Head viaducts. Opening took place for freight trains in August, 1875, and passenger trains in April, 1876. The final cost of the line was £3.6m, some 50% above the projection, an awesome amount for that period.

But in less than 100 years, the 1963 Beeching Report recommended the withdrawal of all the line's passenger services. In 1970 all stations except for Settle and Appleby West closed, with two daily passenger trains each way.

During the 1970s, that peerless British skill of "decline management" meant most freight trains were re-routed onto the electrified West Coast Main Line. Maintenance budgets were slashed and the infrastructure deteriorated.

>>>The line's summit at Ais Gill, north of Garsdale, is 1,169 feet above sea-level. Fast running steam locomotives are limited to a maximum gradient of one in 100, so colossal engineering works were in order. In spite of this, the ascent over the Pennines dictated a 16-mile climb almost continuously at one-in-100.

The writing was on the station toilet wall, so to speak, and closure seemed a foregone conclusion. But in 1981 a protest group, the Friends of the Settle-Carlisle Line (FoSCL), was launched, campaigning against the line's closure before the 1984 official announcement.

The outraged local authorities and rail fans stepped up the anti-closure plan, criticising BR for ignoring its tourism and traffic potential, overlooking its vital role as a West Coast Mainline diversionary route.

A "closure by stealth" campaign by BR was uncovered and all this publicity together greatly boosted traffic. Annual journeys were 93,000 in 1983 when the anti-closure campaign started, but rose to 450,000 by 1989.

Right:
Hellifield Station

Transport minister Michael Portillo finally refused consent to line closure in 1989 and BR was forced to start repairs.

More trains use the line now than at any time in its history. The campaigners' predictions were proved correct. Much freight traffic has been diverted from the congested West Coast Main Line, local passenger traffic has increased and eight stations closed in 1970 reopened. Ribblehead station now boasts a visitor centre.

The S&C's survival is an incredible story of stoic local initiative that matches the original Midland Railway directors' vision. This is people power at its most potent, saving the best of British achievement for the greater longterm good.

HUNGRY FOR STEAM TRAVEL

THE PREMIER WAY TO DINE ON THE LINE OR SNACK ON THE TRACK

Imagine a restaurant that is open for breakfast, lunch and dinner, serving two to five courses of high-quality food at each meal-time. Then imagine that all 168 guests sit down simultaneously at each of these three silver service meals.

And a further 84 customers need serving morning coffee, muffins and pastries, plus afternoon tea and warm scones, clotted cream and jam.

Not only that, but all the food is prepared in a small moving kitchen.

That's the conditions for the catering crew aboard the Liverpool Daily Post & Echo's steam train specials serving passengers in Premier Dining Class and First Class coaches.

Graham Osborne, co-owner and manager of Premier Train Catering, which has the dining contract, claims to be Britain's biggest onboard train caterer.

Above: Alison Roberts who accepted fiancé Andy Morgan's proposal for marriage as they passed Dent Station on the Cambrian Mountain Express
Pictures: Stephen Done

He also works as head chef on the trains, ably assisted by his chefs Danny Currie and Dale Cuthbertson. The 11 dining car stewards are led by Graham's partner Julie Jones, chief stewardess, and Phil Murray, chief steward.

They all start work many hours before the arrival of the passengers they pamper. Graham rose at 2.30am to get breakfast ready and works through to 11pm or later.

"Then we drive home to Harwich," says Graham. They cater onboard charter trains most weekends and also average about two weekday excursions a month.>>>

>>> Graham, who went to sea aged 16, for 19 years, served in the Falklands War on Baltic Ferry. He has cooked on trains for every Royal family member except the Queen.

After joining British Railways in 1989 and working in its charter division, he started Premier Train Catering in 2003 with his business partner Paul Brookes. They employ 15 full-time and 200 part-time staff.

Graham and his crew are assigned to the Royal Scot stock, comprising coaches mainly built in the early 1960s. This is usually stabled at Eastleigh, Hampshire, but will be based at Crewe for the Live Steam from Lime Street summer season.

"Everything is peeled onboard, cooked onboard and washed-up by hand onboard. We have two ovens, 10 hobs, two grills and a hot-cupboard. It's all gas, there's no electricity," says Graham, of his kitchen car which is pushing 50-years-old.

Top right:
Stewardess
Lenka Hrehova

Right: Chef
Danny Currie

"The Fanny Craddocks of this world could not cope with cooking in this galley at 100mph. It's no good squawking 'Where do I plug my blender in?'

"Around 180 premier diners and 80 plus first class passengers is the maximum for a single kitchen car. We need a second fully-staffed kitchen car if more people book."

Chef Danny says: "It takes three hours to prep for dinner. All the meat is carved by hand on the train. On a typical trip for dinner we'd serve 180 plates of roast beef of three portions each."

While Premier Dining Class, with its at-seat Pullman-style service is not cheap, the passenger response is universally fantastic, with nothing but praise for the food and the staff's attentive attitude.

"Well, we do give the lady passengers the table posies when they get off," says Graham modestly.

FIRST

NO SMOKING

BRITISH RAILWAYS

EMERGENCY LIGHTING POINT   1967

1968 AND ALL THAT

OR HOW BRITAIN'S RAILWAY RAN OUT
OF STEAM AFTER 138 YEARS
OF FAITHFUL SERVICE.

THE age of steam power on Britain's mainline railways ended where it began, in North West England. The era closed with the so-called Fifteen Guinea Special (officially charter IT57), the last mainline passenger train to be hauled by steam locomotives on British Rail, on 11 August 1968.

After years of running down its steam power, often operating locomotives in atrocious conditions, BR started its infamous steam ban the following day.

The special farewell rail tour started at Liverpool Lime Street, hauled by LMS Stanier Black Five No 45110 via Rainhill to Manchester Victoria. Replaced by Britannia Class No 70013 Oliver Cromwell (the last steam locomotive to be overhauled by BR), the special departed for Carlisle at via the Settle & Carlisle Railway.

Returning south, two more Stanier Black Fives, Nos 44781 and 44871, double-headed the train back to Manchester Victoria. The final leg saw No 45110 again hauling the train to Liverpool Lime Street.>>>

Spectators pack Lime Street Station as Stanier Black Five No 45110 leaves with British Railways' last mainline steam train on August 11, 1968

>>> Huge crowds turned out to see the train pass, proving the place steam had in people's hearts and their belief nothing would be seen like it again. Spectators beseiged the tracks at stopping places like Rainhill and Ais Gill summit.

After 138 years of steam-hauled trains on our railways, this was a pivotal point in the history of rail travel. From now on all motive power would be by diesel or electric traction.

Those final day locomotives all survived bar one. No 45110 is on the Severn Valley Railway, now named RAF Biggin Hill, but has once returned to Liverpool on the mainline.

No 44871 is being overhauled at the East Lancashire Railway and No 70013 Oliver Cromwell, owned by the National Railway Museum was restored to mainline operation in 2008.

Left: The Lord Mayor of Liverpool waves off BR's last train from Lime Street

Below: The IT57 special halts at Parkside where Liverpool MP William Huskisson was fatally run over by Stephenson's Rocket at the L&MR opening

No 44781 was destroyed during the making of the film The Virgin Soldiers.

The 40th anniversary of the Fifteen Guinea Special was marked by a re-enactment of the tour on Sunday August 10, 2008.

It ran again from Liverpool Lime Street on almost the same route, including No 70013 Oliver Cromwell on the Manchester Victoria - Carlisle leg, but using other Black Fives currently certified for the mainline.

The Fifteen Guinea Special name stuck due to what was regarded by enthusiasts as the outrageously high ticket price (15 guineas = £15 15s 0d). BR said it was responding to the high demand for seats.

Above: More well-wishers cram onto the tracks as the special stops at Rainhill

Top: Young and old experience the footplate of No 45110

Above left: The footplate crew are mobbed for autographs at Lime Street, Liverpool

INDIAN SUMMER OF STEAM

LOOKING BACK TO WHEN STEAM RULED THE RAILS

HIGH heels clacking down platforms to find an empty compartment, the shouts of porters, the scream of safety valves blowing off, the booming but indiscernible Tannoy, the hiss of steam, the squeal of brakes, the guard's shrill whistle and bark of a departing locomotive.

Our smoke-filled, vaulted railway termini were atmospheric real-life stage sets; the scenes for meetings, greetings, happy holiday-makers, callow soldiers on one-way tickets, tearful departures and heart-rending last rites for lovers and relations.

Millions of long-gone brief encounters have evaporated into the ether like the steam which once embraced them.

Liverpool alone boasted three splendid such stations, Lime Street (London & North Western Railway), Exchange (Lancashire & Yorkshire Railway) and Central (Cheshire Lines Committee).

Not to be outdone, Birkenhead was home to the Great Western Railway's Woodside terminus.>>>

Only these carefully tended blooms
lighten the unremitting gloom of
Edge Hill Station as Jubilee class
No 45553 Canada storms past in
this classic early 1950s shot

>>> The trains running between such cathedrals of steam were lifelines upon which the nation's families, commerce and trade depended.

Decades deep as we are into the motorway age, it is easy to forget the importance and all-encompassing effect of the steam railway on our national life.

Modern mass car ownership means we can practically drive wherever and whenever we like. Until the mid-1960s, long distance car travel was along single carriageway trunk roads tediously threading through town centres.

Once the railways provided what now is an almost undreamt of level of public service and access. >>>

Top: A South African Railways coach built by Vulcan Foundary, Newton-le-Willows is loaded at Liverpool Docks

Above: The 100-ton Flying Scotsman is loaded in Liverpool, bound for Boston and a US tour in 1969

Top Right: Great Western Railway flagship loco No 6000 King George V breaks the BR steam ban with a Hereford-Chester special in 1974 at Ruabon

Right: Relaying the West Coast mainline at Winwick

Opposite page Top: Two female enthusiasts discuss the merits of No 7029 Clun Castle, which hauled some of the last Birkenhead-Paddington specials in 1967

Opposite page bottom: No 46208 Princess Helena Victoria blasts up Edge Hill cutting with The Shamrock Express

Top: Formal staff portrait at Crewe Works with mayor after overhaul of last BR steam locomotive Britainnia class No 70013 Oliver Cromwell in 1967

Middle: One of the unusual Fairlie double engines, Earl of Merioneth on the Ffestiniog narrow gauge railway.

Bottom: A Steamy day at the now defunct Southport Steam Centre

>>> Passengers from Liverpool could reach the heart of Snowdonia within a few hours.

In the North West, there was an intricate web of freight lines serving industry, mills and collieries.

Speeds were slower, so dining cars were prolific on all mainline expresses. Sleeping car services radiated out from London to the provinces, with rail centres like Liverpool having their own sleepers to Glasgow.

The premier hotels were developed by the railways. In Liverpool the London Midland & Scottish Railway owned the Adelphi, Exchange and North Western, at Lime Street

Before the war road competition was almost non-existent, plane services were in their infancy and the Royal Mail contracts helped keep the four big private railway companies solvent.

During wartime the homefront and colossal preparations to fight could not have been achieved without rail transport.

After the war, the railways were nationalised in 1948 and in spite of their rundown state achieved the herculean task of getting the nation back on the move and carrying the population on their first holidays since 1939.>>>

Top left: No 6000 King George V get a pull out of Swindon shed for restoration in 1971

Top right : Parriot class No 5515 Carnarvon is named at its namesake town in 1932

Middle Left: No. 46206 Princess Elizabeth hurries the Merseyside Express through Attleborough Staffordshire, June 6 1953. Picture: Clive Mojonnier

Middle Right: A4 class no 4482 Golden Eafle races allong the East Coast mainline.

Right: Britannia class No 70004 William Shakespeare thundering through Bangor Station with the Euston bound relief Irish Mail in 1962. Picture: EN Kneale

Above: City of Bradford hauls The Caledonian in Janurary 1957

Top: Crowds surge around GWR Castle class loco Pendennis Castle
on the Chester Birkenhead Flyer in March 1967 commemorating
closure of Paddington-Birkenhead through trains

Left: Mrs Mercer sprucing up a Merseyside Express
first class carriage in June 1952 at Liverpool Lime Street

Above: Coronation class City of Liverpool was unveiled by LMS chairman Sir Thomas Royden (left) and named by the Lord Mayor, R Duncan French, on September 22 1943

Below: GWR Castle class No 5033 Broughton Castle accelerates over Chester Roodee bridge with the daily Birkenhead-Bournemouth express on October 28 1958

>>> After years of austerity, British Railways tried to rekindle some of the prewar glamour with its named trains on the Lime Street - Euston run, such as The Merseyside Express, Red Rose, Shamrock and Manxman.

Not least we should remember the millions of men and women who dedicated their lives to working for the railways. Often in grim conditions, the shed staff at depots like Edge Hill, Bank Hall and Brunswick daily turned out locomotives to haul the top-link expresses and the humblest goods turns.

Then there were the signal men on whose skills with mechanical equipment everyone relied to ensure speeding trains travelled safely, the track maintenance gangs, the carriage cleaners - the list goes on and on.

So let's take a look at our railways in their pomp before Dr Beeching swung his axe and changed the scene forever.

THE FUTURE OF STEAM AGE

THE LURE OF STEAM WILL LIVE ON FOR YEARS

WHAT of the future for mainline steam? The doom merchants have been predicting its demise ever since the big return in 1974.

As modern trains become faster, vintage steam traction will be under pressure. However, there are always likely to be lines which will not be running at the very high speeds which are the standard for, say, the West Coast Mainline.

New-build steam locomotives like Tornado (right) can run at 90mph making them much more able to fit in with present timetabling demands.

Hopefully, others such as yet half-built Clan class replica Hengist will become a reality.

The huge amount of money now ploughed into the railway heritage scene is indicative of its importance to the nation's tourist industry.

While the privately run preserved lines like the Llangollen Railway, East Lancashire Railway conjure up their own special ambience, there is nothing like an express steam locomotive "stretching its legs" on the mainline.

The success of the Liverpool Daily Post & Echo's Live Steam from Lime Street summer season is proof of how these vintage steam trains have stirred emotions in so many people, far beyond the hardened railway fraternity.

With any luck, we shall be not only to running, but expanding with different locomotives, routes and onboard experiences for years to come, adding to the lustre of this great city of Liverpool and its hinterland.

THE MAN WITH A RAIL-BOUND MISSION

NIGEL DOBBING BRINGS DECADES OF EXPERIENCE TO THE POST AND ECHO STEAM TRAINS

Nigel Dobbing is the man who makes our Live Steam From Lime Street a reality and doggedly shoulders the stress and strain of turning what seem like good ideas into commercial reality.

A former hotelier in railway towns like Doncaster and Swindon, he started his career working on Holland America Line's classic ocean liner Nieuw Amsterdam and he still roams the world looking after his rail tours.

After 10 years as managing director of the Railway Touring Company, he is a past-master at dealing with the multitude of organisations into which the UK's privatised system is now split.

Separate bodies are responsible for track access, station use, locomotive hire, rolling stock and catering.

"It's more complex than other national railway networks such as Argentina, which you would expect to be difficult," says Nigel, who is based in King's Lynn, Norfolk.

"Luckily, I have a terrific staff and dozens of excellent volunteers who help as stewards on the trains."

This year Railway Touring Company will use its exclusive Royal Scot rake of coaches on the Liverpool trips. These handsome 1950s designed British Railways Mark 1 saloons and dining cars were refurbished in April, 2008, by RTC and Riviera Trains for £500,000. The brake coaches can even accommodate two invalide buggies.

"The Royal Scot coaches will take travellers back to the heyday of steam travel and mark a definite up-grade on what we offered last year," says Nigel.

"Last summer more than 6,000 people took one of our summer steam services. With high petrol costs and less holidays abroad, we hope more people will choose steam rail excursions for their days out this year."

Working with the Liverpool Daily Post & Echo, Nigel hopes to build on our 2008 success. Future ideas under consideration include fine dining trains and weekend tours to destinations like the West Highlands.

Nigel Dobbing (left) with Peter Elson discussing steam trains, fine dining and fettling the Royal Scot

Opposite page: No 71000 Duke of Gloucester catches the evening sun as it heads for home

THE ROYAL SCOT